Travels with a Rhymester and more

Keith F. Oldrey

To Gloria. Catwoman

May she never lose her voice?

Keith Oldrey

9/3/18

Published by Grove Horton & Co.
Northampton

First published in 2001 by

Grove Horton & Co.
45 Main Road, Hackleton, Northampton
Telephone: 01604 870189
Fax: 01604 870196
Email: koldrey@compuserve.com

British Library Cataloguing in Publication Data.
A catalogue record for this book is available from the British Library.

ISBN 0-9540514-0-8

Cover Design & Typesetting by The Blayney Partnership, Northampton
Printed & bound by Antony Rowe Ltd, Eastbourne

To my wife Beryl…

…who made this all possible

CONTENTS

CONTENTS

The Author

Keith Oldrey moved from Birmingham to a small Northamptonshire village, (which is the centre of the Universe), for 6 months - "thirty years ago".

His selling abilities in the Steel Industry, have taken him all over the UK and his hobbies of cricket, golf, reading, gardening and holidays have taken him around the world.

He has always had the gift of words (he was once refused permission to kiss the Blarney Stone) and now after several poems published in anthologies, we have brought together a collection of his witty versed thoughts on, places, sports and life's experiences!

Happily married with 3 successful children, he maintains his love of people and an ambition to grow the perfect lawn.

TRAVELS WITH A RHYMESTER
and MORE!!!

BUSINESS CLASS

'We will be flying at 37,000 feet'
Divorced, we look, the countryside is neat
'Gin and Tonic?'
Supersonic
Now it's time to eat
Heathrow to Bilbao, 1000 miles
Pilots biggest problem? Piles!!!
Smoked chicken, poached salmon, kumquats
Cossetted passengers, travelling Club.
Free booze, papers, cabin staff with vision glazed
Serve us, watch us guzzle, never amazed
'Champagne, Sir? Wine, red or white?'
Forget about time, day or night
Airbus 320, flying by wire
Travel, so easy, you cannot tire
And yet, wondering why, how and when
Do I feel, just like a battery Hen!
We're nearly there, just one more need
One last fling is decreed
Duty free, it isn't hard
"Cirrhosis and Cancer, Sir? Pay by plastic card"
Bottle and packet, luxuries and scent
Our trips nearly over,
'Fasten your seatbelts' for final descent

CITY BREAKS Paris

We used to go to France
And heave ho over the gunnel
Now its so much easier
They went and built a tunnel
Off to Paris by Eurostar
So smooth, so fast, it isn't far
Easter in La capitale, it has a joyous ring
Alas, 'twas more like winter, than joyful spring
We saw the Arc de Triomphe, the Eiffel Tower
Enjoyed it all, despite the icy winds and occasional shower
Promenade along the Champs Elysee- things begin to hum
Mais, Mon Dieux, it is expensive just to park your bum
A rest was what we wanted, and a glass of good cheer
But a fiver for a coffee and even more for Beer!
Still culture reigns. Glass pyramid over the Louvre
Sucks the tourists in, better than a Hoover
The Lido in Spring, where the Bluebells unfurl
Certainly feathers, can embellish a girl
My Grandsons views I must impart
When looking at early Italian Art
Our special joke to keep us all happy
"Look Mommy. Angels don't wear a Nappy!
So passed the days. We never got bored
When we took the Eurostar from Waterloo to Gare de Nord

SKYE

Land of swirling mists
Land of kilts and pipes
Land of heather, clinging to the hillsides
Waterfalls and streams pour from the mountain sides
See the evening sun set over Skye
The black mountains softened by the buttercup yellow light
As the green reflect the suns beams
Herons on the shoreline search for their supper
Ungainly steps through the rocks
Then a fish has had his chips
Kingfishers dart by a peat brown stream
Salmon fry and trout are their cream
Whilst Red doe smell the clear air of dawn
As into the clearing, she steps with her fawn
Natures veil of rain and mist
Can never cover the naked beauty of this land
Land of the mountain, Land of the Sea
Land of such beauty, ever calling to me

The Scots

Scottish humour is awful door
Doon and oots and squelchy moor
Laird of the Glen
With points held high
Compare with Glasgie drunks and sigh
Yet no man can be so kind
Or generous in spirit, you will find
Can you really find a fault
To those that invented the single malt????

ITALIAN STUDY

Italy, Land of sunshine and culture
Pizza and Piazza
Paintings and sculpture
Opera, wine fashion and Pasta

Architecture, rich in style
Maria Callas, Roman profile
Ice cream and sun ripe tomato
Simple columns by Palladio

Ferraris and Riva boats
Lake Maggiore and Amalfi coast
Venice, a jewel, lit by lead crystal glass
To sum it all up. Class, class, class

VENICE

The stately homes of Venice
We haven't been there yet
But if you walk across the street
You will get your feet so wet

VERONA

The Theatrico Olympico, a real treat
For on a stage, a backcloth of a classic street
Perspective so perfect, it really is so swell
The only thing that's missing, is the pasta and the smell
Deception of the eye, or tromp d'oeil
Fifteenth Century art form of such joy
That given that, Pride comes before a fall
You could easily, flatten your nose upon this wall

TRAVEL TO GOA

Travel to the land of Goa
Where time stands still, everything slower
Twelve hours flying makes you hazy
But you'll remember the taxis, they're just crazy

Driving like mad, toot, toot, toot
Is it a road, or rapids to shoot?
Drive in the middle, on bends overtake
"Look out" " My God" "For heavens sake!"
Taxis like the Keystone cops
Stop for repairs, crashes and shops
"Yes memsahib, the finest silk"
Dreaming of all the commission, he will milk
Still he will wait, through sun and shower
For very few rupees an hour

Cidade de Goa, our holiday haven
Massages, sport, food and fun
Pleasant rooms for you to run
As malaria tablets took their toll
And you get rid of all you were saving

Stomachs are settled, we're off on a trip
Manpuna market and Anguina hip
Market mysterious, soon entices
With dried fish, fruit and exotic spices
Bargains galore, saris and silks all around
Ray Ban specs for only two pound

But Anguina Hippy Market, I can do without
Just to save the odd rupee
Beggars I could kill and do it for free
Legless men and filthy snake charmers
I think I'd sooner be in the Bahamas
Hippies with Rock cakes
Charmers with snakes
Anguina Beaches
Beggars like leeches
Bangles and beads
All the Worlds needs
But for all that
All the world over, tat is always tat

New Zealand

Forty years I had waited
A dream which had never abated
Now came true with remarkable drama
As dawns light, revealed the magnificent panorama
The Northern islands, emerald jewels in an opal Sea
Tiny bays, isolated farms set in this exquisite filigree

Cheap sheep thrills

Flat Hill Station. A shepherds dream I thought
But the thrill of a lifetime, was what I bought
Acceleration from nought to fifty I am shown
With a whoop and a holler (and a bit of a moan)
We're off, over 100 yards, on water straight at a bank
No where to go, no way to stop
5, 3 litres, foot to the floor
Suddenly I'm not quite so sure
Then the driver spins the wheel
Water and senses start to reel
We've spun around and we're away
Having watered the cattle a mile away
Such good fun, no need to fret
You've had a trip on Flat Hills Sprint jet

South Island

Wellington and on to the ferry
Weather fine and party all merry
Three hours on the Inter islander
She's fitted with a stabiliser
South Islands just astounds
Breathtaking beauty of Queen Charlotte Sound
Sea colours, azure, topaz, turquoise, every hue
Yachts dancing on these waters so blue
Holiday homes - dreams for you and me
Only approachable from the Sea

Lunch Hour

Picton Railway Station, we can say
Should be world famous for the buffet
Delicious fish bites and teryaki chicken
Everyone maximises when they're picking
Behind the curtain, a train to announce
Best keep quiet, before we pounce
As soon as it is over
On the National Dish - Kiwi Fruit Pavlova

West Coast

Greymouth and south, we all feel
Is just too beautiful, to be real
Seas crashing on the beach that started
From Antarctic icebergs, long departed
Jagged rocks piercing silvery sand
Unspoilt by Mans desecrating hand
Pancake rocks in sculptured layers
Point heavenward, like Gods own prayers
Miles and miles of untouched strand
Backed by silver fern, rain forest land

'WHAT ER' FEARFUL TRIP

Shotover Jet Boat - where grown men shiver
As they're hurled down the river
Screaming along, past canyons sheer walls
360 degree turns, that soak your balls!!

Rain like needles in your face
A good half an hour, up and down you race
With the adrenaline coursing free
You get off like a drowned rat
Dying for a PEE !!!!!!!!!

Milford Sound
sleeping tourists

Best remembered by Knobs Landing (love the pun)
Descending from Japan and Korea for 3 days fun
Pouring from the coaches on the run
Laughing and chattering with great glee
Standing in the queue for a pee
Waiting patiently with camera and recorder
Mr Wang and Mr Chan from Chinese border
Three day tours, never a minute late
But in the loo they proliferate
Though they may enter on their own
With camera, mack and mobile phone
When they come back thro the door
I swear there appears to be more and more
Milford Sound - Eighth wonder of the World
Your beauties will soon enfold
And the sand flies - carnivorous little beasties
Will compete with hordes from the Far Easties

TOURING NAUSEA

Milford Sound, scenery so grand
On awesome scale Nature planned
Dolphins, brown fur seals on hand
Yet though the scene is more than fair
Somehow, I cannot raise a care
Even if the mountain does rear
A mile high from sea to sky
And beautiful waterfalls, greet your eye
Still I feel a little morose
Could it be 'Sightseeing overdose'

'LOOK OUT HILL'

Dunedin, where statues, past and future
In bronze and marble
Now proclaim, in spray can paint
The lack of Janet Hamilton's virtue
Male ego spurned
Readily turned
To graffiti for mindless relief

MORIEKA STONES

Rocks like eggs well rounded
For millions of years they have astounded
Looking like something from outer space
Imagine the look upon the face
When these six foot diameter eggs were laid
No wonder kiwi birds, flightless are made

KAWARAN BRIDGE
140ft of pant filling air

Bungy jumping - pretty nifty
You can go free, if over sixty
Or ladies if you bare your lumps
Used not to pay for their jumps
Surely a moral to this tail
But just for once, words do fail!!!

In memoriam

Welcome stranger to the Land of the Long White Cloud
A country of which, you must be so proud
Clean and keen on conservation
Idyllic beauty and preservation

Friendly people extol its charms
Difficult to believe, their call to arms
When they heard their Mother Country call
Tragic, that so many, from so few, should fall

Yet Mothers rules, have done them proud
And not enough people to make a crowd
Keep this land of peaceful scene
Soft, warm, gentle and so serene

FIJI

FIJI - please read forms carefully
When filling out, immigration form
All negative is the norm
Do you carry semen? In which way?
God I hope they don't take my balls away
At least not until after the holiday!!!

PARADISE

Palm fronds, whisper in the evening breeze
Golden sunset descends into the seas
Mynah birds chattering overhead
Whilst frogs appear on putting green
Is it real or a Gaugin scene?

Curried chicken, tres magnifique
Served in coconut shell, quite unique
Wine enough to fulfil your wishes
From Oz and Kiwi, complimenting these dishes
All served with smile and Fijian shirt
By dark Adonis in Polynesian skirt
Finally the answer to a Maiden's Prayer
A dark skinned Evian water sprayer
To save the skinning of the shoulder
And keep the desires just off smoulder

FLYING 747

You have to come to the conclusion
That though it's nice. Travel is an illusion
Processed down a plastic tube
Ears subjected to a constant hum
Seats that do nothing for your bum.

Where have you been, what did you see
The only one who cares is ME

The cramp, the pain in arthritic knee
Honolulu, New Zealand and Fiji
May have been wonderful to the eye
But here and now, up in the sky
I dream of comfort and my own bed
The finest Paradise to rest my head

Kicking Horse Pass

I wonder, how he decided
That the waters of the Rockies divided
Was it the kick in the ass
In Kicking Horse Pass
Giving him the idea specific
Waters to the right - Atlantic
Waters to the left - PACIFIC!!!!!

YO Ho we go down to Field
Over Kicking Horse Pass, all is revealed
As trains climb mile long in a spiral
Defeating Nature by means environmental
Grain wagons carrying 70 tonne
For the CPR it must be fun
Like a mule with a steady pull and little brain
Hauling this 15,000 ton train

Chateau Louise

On Emerald Lake, natural bridges
Carved over eons by melting snow
Whilst on the lake at Chateau Louise
Ice melts thin, under Springs hot sun
And a thousand windows gaze sightless
Upon glacial splendours

Sulphur Mountain 7,500ft

Superb, the word for the drama
Revealed, the wonderful mountain panorama
Viewed from Sulphur Mountain summit
Like a map, it looks so neat
Spread beneath your feet
The gondola may be a bit of a squeeze
But certainly easier on the knees
Though on the piste, you could ski
The Gondola is more my cup of tea
And the snackbar, where we can tell the tale
Of how we dined on 'Beaver Tail'

KAMLOOPS

Kamloops trains give a toot
When transporting the Ginseng root
Keeping Chinkies velly fit
Here grown under black shaded bit.
Though very expensive to start to grow
A Splendid return it does show
So if you can grow it, you may whoop and holler
And expect a good return to the dollar

BUTCHART GARDENS

Butchart Gardens, bloom in the May
By scent and sight a wondrous display
As through the flower beds we wended
Each one so immaculately tended
Visitors here from every nation
Awed and inspired by Mrs Butchart's creation

THE EMPRESS HOTEL

Empress Hotel, Victoria's Queen
Over the years, what sights have you seen
Kings Queens Presidents and Czar's
Now in 1997, it's more Ma and Pa's
Your Bengal Lounge, regal in Oak
Offers civilised drinking, but not for the broke
Coffee and beer will soon slake our thirst
Then Kipling's Terrace Buffet and maybe we'll burst

Osprey

Okenhagen Lake
Where Osprey take
The fish and fly
Off across the sky
(or was it an Okogogo)
Canada's version of Loch Ness

Commuting

Kelowna left via the new spur
Four hours drive does not deter
Vancouver commuters as they flee
To this Lake far from the sea

Then to Merritt, nestling in the hills
Nothing here to require any pills
So we climb through trees so dense
Past the worlds most expensive fence

Lunchtime calls and we mope
Around the pleasant streets of Hope
Where finally, we meet
In timber carved so discreet
Chip & Old Timer, Cougar & Bear
And many other friends to share Hope is a place of some fame
When the moving picture folks came.
Yes. Sylvester Stallone first came good
Physically demanding in 'First Blood'
Yet though good manners, you may be taught
You only got an extras job, if you were short
So Hope was displayed across the nation
Do you remember the explosion at the petrol station!!!!

But we're still following the path of the train
Now we enter on to Vancouvers alluvial plain
Soft fruits grow, making merry
In this good soil, ideal for rasp and loganberry

Then it's a journey out to sea
Travelling on a large ferry
Where the island scenery is a delight
Spotting the Bald Eagles in full flight

Finally Victoria for drink and nosh
Hotels fine and suburbs posh
Lovely houses, parks and yachts
Definitely not the place for the have-nots

CHEMAINUS

Now the Islands tourist trap
When the logging finished
The Murals put it, on the map
We walked its streets and no one could moan
Especially if tempted by the Welsh Teahouse scone

THE LONG WALK

Swinging places, I have seen
But Capolino is real mean
A walk across this 450 ft suspension
Does a lot for hypertension
An if you don't jump and meet your Fate
They give you proof, by certificate

Then on to Salmon hatchery
Where we all try
To spot the fry
Of Chinook, Choko and Sockeye
Whilst from rocky crag, fishermen took
Steelhead trout from this more than babbling brook

VANCOUVER

Grouse Mountain 1 mile high
Is the best place, Vancouver to espy
Snow and choppers, Beaver Tails
Heatstroke leaves us hanging on the rails
As Bald Eagle flights we simulated
All returned, hot, tired but elated

Such a pleasure, such a delight
Architectural vision and foresight
Providing buildings, so practical and exciting
Great to look at and still inviting
A city so pleasing to the eye
Each glass reflection merging with the sky
Vancouver a delight, individual yet a combination
With Nature's beauty, mountain sea and parks
A monument to the strength of the people
who have made Canada
Long may they continue to see the whole concept
Stanley Park, donated to all colours and creeds
Seven Kilometres of cycle track surrounding
Trees and flowers, a wonderful Aquarium
Play area, Painters, Restaurants
Walking around the Lost Lagoon
Watching Herons and Raccoon
Rollerbladers and Sandy Beach
The City Centre almost within reach
So we enjoy Vancouver's pleasures
Only our feet object to our leisure
Vancouver we will return

THE FLIGHT

Night flight
Nutmeg grated eyeballs
Greet the dawn
Our giant bird follows ancient watercourses
Across the deserts of Iran
Can people live down there?
Yet tiny fields show it is so
India now and precious water changes
The still brown earth
Rivers and their verdant accompaniment
Meander across the plains
Water brings civilisation
Straight roads link communities
Still our giant bird follows the ancient paths
Following mans struggles along the easiest ways
Nine hours gone, one to go
Where are we?
Oh Calcutta keep your hair on
Seas of jade, islands of umber
Strange land patterns
Jigsaws cut by rivers searching for the sea
Mysteries we will never know as rubber kisses concrete
And we stretch our legs so thankfully
Reaching for the lockers
Certain that 400 people can disembark in 2 minutes
When it took half an hour to load

BANGKOK

Hardly Elysian fields
Concrete and rubbish soon revealed
As we pass through miles of squalor
In mans pursuit of the mighty dollar

Car and lorry, pick up truck
Exhausts belching, quite a shock
Whilst motorbikes in hundreds fight
To be the first away, from the light

1600 baht - £3 per day
we are told is daily pay
Cars forever in respray
Help economy on its way

Yet Mercedes and Jags show that riches
Are there for those who watch from ditches
Filling bellies with the fire
That one day to a Rolls Royce they will aspire

THE ORIENTAL HOTEL

Who put the fold in the toilet roll
And when do you think they do it?
Soft tissue origami
Nearly drives you barmy
When folds appear between each visit

Can it be true
Are there cameras in each loo
And a full time folder just to view it
For there are slippers by the bed
And it must be said
Every item you could possibly wish for
Bits and pieces by the score.
All these things are fundamental
When your stopping at The Oriental

CHANG MAI

Chang Mai and Mr Ting
Here to show us everything
Small in stature, but big in heart
I am sure, he'll play his part
And every local craftsman show
So lets get up and go go go

Umbrellas from rice paper made
Painted, lacquered and brilliantly displayed
Silk worms live on the mulberry tree
The finest gossamer spinning free
Cloth so rich, woven soon
From this egg shaped cocoon
Lacquerware factory where trays of bamboo
Are hand painted on lacquer black
You'll not see better on a Guardsman's shoe
Then sapphires, diamonds and rubies we're shown
Exotic jewellery that will be flown
To excite the eye of Arab sheik
Or perhaps to make
A reward for Japanese Geisha or Brooklyn belle
For we look and think 'What the hell'
Such a terrible waste
To use such beauty in such bad taste

Then elephants and buddhas we see made
In every colour and type of jade
German ladies worry, should it come to pass
That their expensive jade elephant, could be made out of glass

Chairs and furniture made out of teak
Any object you can seek
Crafted from solid teak
Yet cutting teak trees, is now banned
Where therefore was this timber found
And if you ship it in broken down bits
What recompense, if it splits
For though I asked and I certainly tried
They couldn't guarantee that it was properly dried

RAFTING

A bamboo raft has many poles
It only goes, downhill
It floats so gently over shoals
And never makes you ill
And what is more in your coolie hat
You are captain of the craft
And you will never sink
Floating down the Mae kong
Tickles us quite pink

THE GOLDEN TRIANGLE

Le Meridien at Baan Boraan
From your bedroom, you can scan
Thailand, from its tourists getting rich
For Myanmar life's a bitch
With opium and tiger skins
Staying poor, for its sins
Meanwhile Laos folks just don't wave
Not surprising for they must crave
For peace and stability
Life now is more than a bowl of rice
And cats foreskin with your whisky
They'd rather have a mobile phone
Than the scrapings of a rhino's bone
But methinks a giant leap
Will be needed, for they're half a sleep

BURMA

Round the market we can see
Eggs, injected with spice and honey
Bones and horn and tiger's genitalia
Dried, preserved in case yours should fail ya
For Eastern men, get very frisky
When they mix it with their whisky

Doi Suthep

Doi Suthep Temple gives you a thrill
If and when you climb up the Hill
For this trip to an Elephants grave
You need fitness and to be brave
For hairpin bends, this super climb
Helps me with my little rhyme
306 steps to keep you fit
Doesn't help the knees a bit
Yet pagodas huge beyond belief
Covered in square inches of gold leaf
Bells of steel, bells of bronze
Sing melodious tones for the ones
Who worship Buddha for their relief

TEA, TIFFIN & RAIN
Must be 5.30 again

The lagoon dissolved into a mist
Created by the tropical storm
Ground previously kissed
By Sun, now damp and leaves forlorn

Rattan blinds on the Ruan Thai
Try to keep the rains at bay
Yet suddenly, all the mystery of the East
Was there, exposed in this tropical feast

Rain to fill the paddy field
Rain to grow the rice
Rain that falls and never yields
Rain that does entice

For I could throw my clothes off
Dance naked in the rain
For the storm and rain has a primeval beat
It hammers in my brain

The crow does call
Mynahs sing
And dust that settles on the street
Is quickly washed away

Not long the rain
There was no storm
A Deluge impression on my brain
In words so quickly drawn

THE GECKO

Hello gecko, have you heard
The calling card of a hunting bird
Is his cry an alarm call
To keep you pressed against my wall

THE DAWN CHORUS

A golden orb rises over the trees
Skies alive with sound
Thais starlings, yellow heads, impersonate the world
Pigeons coo or are they frogs
Kingfishers wait to catch their breakfast
Crows caw, azure bodied blackheaded birds fly from tree to tree
No wind, just a cheerful cacophony of bird and frog calls
Yet even here the sounds of traffic intrude
As the needs of the hotel complex are fed
By put - puts and taxis and vehicles
Sawadee krup - Good morning world

The badge tells all

Supaporn and Pyjamas, Sui Tai and Pun
Names of joy to give our tongues such fun
Yet as we have Smiths, we can see
That Thais largest family
Are the Trainee

PATHONG BEACH

Then to the High St, where we saw
'T' shirts and watches from ceiling to floor
Scruffs of the world appear to unite
On these streets of Whores and Transvestite
Yet this line is not quite fair
For families having fun also share
The bright lights, bargains, lobster and seafood there
No danger signs, nothing to fear
Just holiday frolics, fed by Singha beer

CASE HISTORY

Bought brand new in pristine condition
Almost a holiday tradition
Yet soon they face the living hell
Of aircraft holds and carousel.
Samsonite and Delsey
From Leeds and Chelsea
Are portered, humped and lumbered
Emptied, repacked and room numbered.
Holiday makers
Are their takers
Full of shirts, dresses and knickers
Owned by Farmers and City slickers.
Oh such a bore
This daily chore
Packed and bulging
Zips are not holding
Finally exploding
Strapped,scarred and bent
Once again heaven sent.
Then fifty weeks quite ecstatic
Gathering dust up in the attic!

THE MAPLE TREE

The maple tree is very neat
With slender bough and syrup sweet
And when it comes up to the fall
Comes the finest trick of all
For then with leaves of red and yellow
He really is a splendid fellow
But by the time of trick or treat
His splendours lie around his feet
Then, Oh then, he becomes a pain
With slippery path and blocked up drain
But all in all, we must agree
He really is a splendid tree !!

Plymouth
Fast food to go

Weather vane Gallery on the Pier
Fish of all kinds from the mere
Scallops, scrod or Lobster roll
You're bound to find something to fill the hole
The only trouble, I'm confessing.
When it comes to dressings
I'm guessing!!!!
Honey Mustard, Dill, Italian or French
Quotes the buxom wench
I feel that I could write a ballad
For all the companions of a salad
One thing sure, we'll never beat it
Our stomachs cannot defeat it
But we may get the final say
For they will box it and we may take it away
And so we face it for another day

Shelburne Museum
Bennington, Vermont

Shelburne Museum and its history
Simply revealing the mystery
Of Vermont and American ways
Reaching back to Pioneer days

Sidewheel steamers and canoes
Transport for cross-country blues
Toys and quilts and butter moulds
The taste of the past soon unfolds

See the circus parade, acrobats and horse
Railway trains, telegraph by Morse
Cradles, glassware, textile looms
Antiques decorate all the rooms

Monuments, lighthouse, and covered bridge
Tobacco Indians, figureheads and primitive fridge
Each item so revealing
History reborn, alive with feeling

Beech Cabin, trophies on the wall
Better be careful, should they fall
Wonderful bronzes and Indian Art
But for me, the special part
Was the memorial poem on the Wall

Manhattan splendour with Degas transported
By the Webbs, so well supported
Objects primitive, objet d'art
History from near and far

Founded in Nineteen forty seven
This living piece of historical heaven
Did the founders wake up one night
And decide to create, the first Webb site?

SS Ticonderoga

How could I forget the SS. Ticonderoga
Now free from trials by wind and rain
Crossing daily - Lake Champlain
Five Miles across the land she travelled
All her rotten timbers unravelled
Now repaired to all her Glory
Proudly she sits and tells her story
Of day trippers from Boston and New York
Of flappers and trappers and all their talk
Now on grassy meadow she will lie
No watery grave for her to die
Once more, cash she will earn
This new found Queen of Shelburne

KANCEMANGUS HIGHWAY
= the fearless ones

Mt. Willy, can this be true?
But never mind, we love the view
They have some ducks that never get fat
The price of food makes sure of that

White Mountain, good place for prayin'
If you go up on funicular train
The Chateaux Hotel, where we're told
Governments decide the price of Gold

So we take the Mountain way
Notching up 'Notches' on the way
Glorious autumn colours on either side
Shown to us by Linda, our guide'

Mt Washington, you can see
Is the place to go, if you want to ski
They have the locals on the run
They like the money, but not the fun
Maybe they don't call it Lune Park for nothing

Conway Town, where you can find
Old railway trains and games of 'Dirty Mind'
Then they showed us 'Echo Lake'
And suddenly shopping was a mistake
Eagles challenged by hang gliders
Watch the vertigo - less climbers
As with careful step they trace
A tortuous crossing of a sheer granite face

EPITAPH

The pictures came back, and what did we find?
They did not compare with those in my mind
Have our eyes dimmed? Can I go back
To disagree the results with Mr Kodak

Different films I tried, Fuji, Kodak and York
With holiday companions, I must talk
Are we being taken, for photographic nerds
Or perhaps colours are better in memory and words

Soon in the albums they will go
To bored friends and neighbours we'll show
Then the shelf, will support these reminders and their cost
Fading memories of places, and friends never lost

The party's over

Time to go and tempers fray
As homeward, we must stray
Have you got the tickets? luggage labels all marked?
Of course Dear. Getting more and more narked
Women are always perfect
Men San faire rien
In all the worlds dialects
The women, tell you when
We've had a shower, the bags all packed
We know we will all be tracked
Across the oceans, across land and seas
Plotted as we go through longitude degrees
Jet lag to confront us
With meals at 35,000 feet
We'll just keep journeying across the globe so neat
Strangers we will talk to, and all of them we can greet
For English fortunately is the language they all speak!
The party ís over, we have a tan, we've had no gippy tummy
Now we must return to work and work
To pay that plastic money

WILL IT BE LIKE THIS

I am so glad, that of King Neptune's daughters
Stephanie was the one that taught us
To enjoy the pleasures of the dive
To scuba, and so survive
That I may see the wonders of the deep
Like a dream when we're asleep
Floating suspended in watery space
Seeing coloured fish, shark, squid with carapace
All revealed, this underwater heaven
Another world in perpetual motion
This wondrous clear, Indian Ocean.

Cabaret

Jambo Manbo acrobats
Gymnastic aristocrats
Basket ball coaches would sigh
For a 2 metre supporter lifting three men high.

African Sounds were really humming
When you listen to their drumming
Dances made with such precision
You hardly felt the circumcision.

The Goods

Elephants, carved in ebony, very expensive
Bargains that may be representative
You can get busts in teak
That may cause a ripple
When you see the sort of nipple
That could take out the eye
Or feed the tallest leanest Masai.

The gauntlet

Silver sand along a scimitar beach
Sand bar and reef, just out of reach
For we must run the Hawkers gauntlet
Soapstone and carvings we must breach
With white socks and hours of barter
For the bargain which is both parties Kismet
Safer yet, is the rule
To stay and drink Tuskers by the pool.

Holiday

Dawns sunlight of palest gold
Zephyr breezes from the sea
So another glorious day enfolds
It really is, my cup of tea.

Apache

Oh my god, what have I done
Getting a haircut, sounds like fun
But no one told me and I went quite pale
When they cut my hair with a flail!
Not a problem, I thought of that
The rest of the holiday, I'll wear a hat

Bugs galore

Dudus to the left, Dudus to the right
Dudus in the morning, Dudus in the night
Dudus that sting, Dudus that bite
Only Johnson's spray, puts all Dudus to flight

SHIMBA LODGE

Shimba Lodge a shattering experience
FF & MM'd after our jungle walk
Only the coffee provided enough adrenaline to climb into bed
Where cocooned by our mosquito net
We died to the frogs chorus.

Room 19 a Shimba suite
Bed bath and lounge so neat
Listen as the cicada call
Accompanied by the waterfall.

Watch a million jewels in the night
Moths all dancing in floodlight
Silver trees in stark relief hold cicada
Keeping the night at bay with their aria
Mongoose play and fish on the sandy banks
And the heat presses on our eyelids
Sending us to sleep.

A red squirrel helps himself to tea
A fish eagle in a silver tree.
Water monitor lizards in single file
Slip in the water like a crocodile.

A full moon lights the sky
I think but cannot even try
To find in any way
A better spot to celebrate my birthday
Whilst mongoose frolic on the sand
And cicada provide the band.

We're off on safari, camera ready
But how exactly do you hold it steady
A spider suddenly provides a treat
But leaving a lady standing on her seat.

Elephant and Savannah buffalo
Putting on their finest show.
Just 5 giraffe, quite a surprise
Their coats in the jungle a perfect disguise

Sable antelope,with horns so long
Though with a kid there is something wrong
Then we see a baboon at last
And back to the lodge for breakfast

Just one animal I forgot to mention
I wouldn't have missed it for a pension
A king of birds for us to see
It was a crowned eagle up a tree.

An experience never to be forgotten.
For we were spoilt something rotten
With food suitably gourmet
We will return - another day.

A f r i c a   i n   t h e   r a w

Today, we have a pilot trip
To an African village and then a snake pit
I only hope it will be hip
And despite the rigours we remain fit.

Up country its still real bad
For tourists it is quite sad
Safari buses stuck for hours
In torrential rain and no showers.

People can write a book
On the way they live,talk and look.
Yet one fact we can shout out loud
No matter creed or country
Of your home your always proud
Whether brick, stone timber or wattle and mud
Its yours and makes you feel so good.
From New Zealand to Kenya all the people share
The pride, it's in their look.
At their home, bits and pieces and all the work it took.

We were embarrassed that we were rich in worldly goods
Yet we could not compete with the kindness and foods
Given to us by these simple people.
To offer sustenance to a stranger
We all learnt a lesson today
But just how can we repay
For money corrupts and there are too many with too little.
Yet they are happy, the children play and laugh
They work and they are free, unlike European children
Imprisoned by monetary and computerised conditioning.
Which is best, poverty, freedom and disease
Or materialism, television, agoraphobia and distrust.

To be continued, I wish I had the answers.

African hazards

We came to Kenya for relaxation and fun
Promises of gourmet food,white sands and burning sun
We were going to the jungle, on the Equator
So for every likely problem, we had to cater.
Plasters,jungle juice fly spray and Diacalm
Would surely protect us and keep us free from harm
But alas alack, we had to admit defeat.
When wee nasty beasties came walking out of the meat.

Thanks to Barry Preece, wherever you are

When you ate your sandwich, I know that you were pained
But remember the maggot, now he never complained
When he saw Beryl's teeth, bearing down on his head
He just panicked and ran to the end of the bread
Now I know that you were hungry
And we know that needs must
But he was shaking with fear on the edge of your crust
So feel no remorse when this story you tell
Just remember that maggots may have feelings as well.

1940 - 1950

Three stumps, chalked upon the wall
The skipper - owner of the bat and ball
Battles recalled and Tests replayed
Compton and Edrich, centuries made
Playing until the sun went down
In passage, road and on waste ground
No TV then to spoil the play
Imaginations soared
No time to be bored
Each stick, a rifle or a gun
Each lamp post hid an Indian or the Hun
Adventures waited at every turn
No time to walk, only run
From five to ten, life was such fun

The stumps chalked upon the wall
The bowlers end - a coat
We played from dawn to dusk
With a tennis ball, bought for a tanner
The bat, a length of deal
Until, we got a PROPER bat
With three springs!
Bringing the responsibility of being skipper
No questions, no lends, the divine rights
For when he goes home, the innings ends
The season from Spring to Conker time
Then trollies took a turn and waste tips
Where scoured for pram wheels and axles
Football days were brief
A 10-0 defeat embarrassed 'The Head'
And sent us early to our bed
Tomorrow another day, as arms linked
We trotted around the playground
In search of Zorro, our hearts torn
By Flicka and Lassie
Begone childish memories - the happiest days of our life

National Poetry Day, Radio 2, 10th October 1997

GOLF - SLOW TORTURE BY HANDICAP

Golf is such a silly game
The less you play it - the greater the Fame
But not alas for your average punter
Who stalks the long grass, more like a hunter
He really isn't playing at all
Half the time, He's looking for his ball.
Head always moving, (if not hanging in shame)
The ball stays still, so the player's to blame
As more and more strokes we amass
Mainly playing from the longest grass
Tempers flaming and words quite blue
Are you sure, this is, the game for you?
Then, just one shot, that you do not thin
And look - Your nearest the pin
Bringing the fame, that you really seek
Ensuring your return, and the dream
That you will do better - next week!!!!!!

P.S.

PS: Dear Ed - 'What a to do'
Hearing my poem on Radio 2
My apologies, for the 'poetic rhyming slip'
Which in the bud, I really must nip
I have to admit, that where I come from
Which originally was just outside Brum
Phonetically, we have problems with our 'grass'
So now its off to Church and may be mass
Where perchance it may come to pass
That finally
I will recognise my donkey from my ass !!!!!!!!

THE LESSON

Swing it slow and you will smile
As that ball goes many a mile
Head quite still and eye on the ball
You'll be back in the Club, with stories tall

Swing too fast, or move your head
You may as well have stopped in bed
Where you may get more satisfaction
Than the damn and blast of a golf reaction

Still golf, can give a lot of pleasure
A walking aid to a lifetimes leisure
Exercise and relief to the soul
When that silly ball, goes straight in the HOLE!

WORLD CUP MANIA

Mania grips the entire World
As we see on TV
Every nations flag unfurled
Which country will climb the ladder
On verdant sward, kicking a bladder?

Cards, yellow and red
The referee, the man to dread
Bringing dishonour - let no man scoff
For the rest of your life, if sent off
Yet others score goals and reach for the skies
Forever a hero, in their fans eyes

Hero and villain, the scene is set
Ninety minutes, the play, the world the stage
TV Viewers of every age
From every dominion
Watching, so certain in their opinion

So football and each team of eleven
Seek for Glory and a place in heaven
Beer will be drunk, blood will be spilt
By men in trousers and in kilt
Patriots all, in the name of sport
In this TV Arena
We all are caught

UP WITH A ROAR

Balloon magic, we simply adore
It's not flying, gliding or even a soar
Ethereal progress, I have to declare
A simple lifting into the air

Dogs aware, give chase and bark
At this wonderful ballooning lark
As smoothly to the heavens, we ascend
With dotty pilots, completely round the bend

Flying silently, over Ordinance Survey pattern
All revealed in 3D fashion
An occasional roar to maintain the heat
England's countryside, glorious and neat

Dawn flight we're told is the best
When folks rush out in nightie and vest
Unaware, that from our heavenly seat
All is exposed, from cleavage to feet!

Alas our journey, too soon was over
A bumpy landing in the clover
Balloon deflated and champagne to sup
Lending a hand, to pack things up

Such an experience, to savour and store
Like a drug, we could take more and more
It certainly wont take much urgin
To make another date with this Virgin

OLD GAMES FOR OLDER PLAYERS

Masochists unite
For I think I'm right
In finding the games, that will send
You all, completely round the bend

GOLF and BRIDGE, you will find
Are games cerebral, of the kind
Requiring practice, precision to besot
Your need to become a robot

So we read, practice and learn
New clubs we try and money we burn
Knowing that, should we double
We could finish in all kinds of trouble

Waiting for those words of dread
From your partner, who will confirm
The terror locked within, like a worm
'You know you shouldn't lift your head'

Yet as we grow older, we simply don't care
As new delights we learn and share
With aches and pains in shoulder and knee
Anything is better than watching TV.

BRIDGE NIGHT

Take the cards, and well them make
Penny a point is the stake
Acol instructions, ready to follow
Where would we be, without Victor Mollo

An aces worth just points four
Short suit, worth one point more
Who will win the important contract
What is this feeling, it makes me sick
Up on your luck and down by one trick
I called one heart
You came back a spade
Is there no suit in which we can trade?

Play No Trumps, renege never
If done, friendships can sever
The hand commences, the dummy laid
Truths of the bidding all displayed
Yes we make it, plus one over
Vulnerable now, we could be in clover
But miscount the trumps and you can suffer
Damn, we went and lost the rubber

The evening passes, such good fun
The cards were good, we had a run
"Your place next week? What time?
My turn to bring the wine"
"OK leave the door ajar"
We'll look forward to travel one bridge too far!!

SHORT MAT BOWLS

Short Mat bowlers, reign supreme
With Woods and wicks and measures in between
Up and down the Mats, they go
Immaculate greys and whites, all on show

Social and lively, it does you good
Provided you keep away from that wood
Lots of chalk when Jack gets kisses
Never mind, we wont tell his missus

Fun and games, in Village Halls
Ringing with laughter, but serious sport
Wherever Short Mat Bowls is taught
Senior Citizens all out to play
Enjoying their time, the short mat way

BATSMAN

To every point of any compass
Speeds the leather from willow dispatched
With grace and power
Some helped on their way
Others with delicacy, deflected
Leather meeting the full face
Dispatched as fast as it had come
Oe'r grass and thro' the air
To such despair from bowler
Who with renewed vim
Tries in vain, to dig them in
Only to see, according to the book
The ball flow to the boundary
By pull and cut, drive and hook
So the glory of the game we defend
When watching from the batsman's end

THE STUMPER

The keeper crouches
Seeing all
Totally involved
Poised waiting
For the faintest snick
The bowlers tempting slower ball
To pull the batsman from his crease
The miss, the take, the appeal
One swift movement to remove the bails
Seldom rewarded by blinking umpire
Yet satisfying and compensation
For the hours crouching
The bent fingers
Missing teeth
Bruises
The sciatica still to come
Pains removed by a memories smile

CRICKET

Summer comes and flannelled fools
Pass the sunshine hours away
Far from jobs, with paper and tools
Glorious cricket, we pretend to play

No game provides such excuses
So many ways, to get yourself out
The drops, the runs, the seamed bruises
The appeals, that loud Howzat.

The wrong decisions
Doubtful catches
Home team bias, raises suspicions
The draws that end most matches

The ego trip, as crowds applaud
The batsman, with his sword
As bowler tries to defile
His territory with leather missile

Returning to Pavilions with a cheer
Your only thought, a long cool beer
Acknowledged by your team mates
As they await, their unknown fates

This glorious game of brain and brawn
Played on concrete and velvet lawn
Cricket, game of both beauty and attrition
My Summer love, my Church, my Mission

NAUGHTY THOUGHTS

Ear lobe licking
Starts
Hearts
Ticking
Tiny hairs lifting
Back of neck, outer thigh
Palpitations, sigh
Basic instincts, love and fear
Darling, I lend you, my ear

RICH DREAMS

There's an awful lot of comfort in a breast
Over many, many years they've stood the test
Every curve, every shape, we love them all
There is nothing, we would alter
As we kneel, before their altar
There's an awful lot of comfort in a breast

Now they fit into your hand, just like a glove
We find them very pleasant, when making love
For just above the waist
They are very good to taste.
Yes there's an awful lot of comfort in a breast

Like the down on an eider's nest
You can compare a chest
And they're just as comfortable to lie on
Then what is more than fair
Is that they come as a pair
Yes there is an awful lot of comfort in a breast

WOMENS INSTITUTE REVEALS ALL

W.I. Ladies have us in fits
Showing off hats and glimpsing their bits
Votes for Jerusalem, home made jam
Lace, knitting and home cured ham
These will never be the same
Now we know their proper game
All those thanks from floor to Chair
Gone forever now they're bare
Rosemary Connolly has had a fright
When the WI competes on cellulite!
Now your finest parts you show
What we, mere males, need to know
Is how many girls can we thrill
Hiding our jewels, behind an electric drill?
Yet one thing is sure, we see with clarity
You can't do enough for a worthy charity

More Thoughts
Writing across the ages

Years ago, in ancient times
Man scribed rocks with animal signs
Then papyrus and hieroglyphics
Designed pyramids quite specific

Years went by and paper with quill
The well of knowledge, did fulfil
Typewriter, telegraphed news (copy dated)
Couldn't keep the worlds appetite sated

Soon, we reached another phase
As radio waves bounced across the ether
There was no need for copperplate
The written word had met its fate

Then television removed all the strictures
NEWS STORIES, complete with pictures
Truth in view for every eye to see
No pulling punches or matter of opinion

No need now to fly by jet
Its faster now, by internet
Fax is great, but bound to fail
When compared with the benefit of e-mail

Yet still we write and pray in vain
That one piece of work will perhaps remain
One poem, one book. A literary masterpiece, to show
That finally at last, man has overcome his own ego !!!

Poets lament

Tell me, tell me. How, as I lie here in my bed
Can I get rid of the ideas. Thoughts that race around my head?
Such talents wasted, brilliant ideas, so rare
Yet when I awake, they're no longer there

Now, here I am, I am the Tutor
Connected to my little computer
Could we only catch the train
Of words, charging thro' my brain

Poetry flowing like a sonata
Majestic, as in a cantata
Soft and lilting, a dictionaries ballet
The Mozart of words, I try to say

But alas how my words fail
If compared with the song of a nightingale
As difficult to catch indeed
As the melodious sound of a clarinets reed

A birds eye view

Starlings sit, on telephone lines
Traffic queues, double white lines
Pavements cracked and litter abound
Graffiti now, that fails to astound
Countryside once, now bulldozer rent
Covered by brick, rubbish and cement
Some grass uncut, some gardens thrive
But cars are polished on every drive
Shopping and factories, start to sprawl
Yet without a car, no good at all
Behind every window a TV set
Computers searching Internet
For news, education, shopping, games to beat
Played by children, afraid to play upon the street

DAD'S LAMENT

Mothers gone to W.I.
Flowers to arrange, new menus to try
Village Halls from floor to rafter
Splendid with chat, ringing with laughter
Admiring the new dress, hearing the news
Sympathy at illness, practical advice
I think the ladies, have got it real nice
For me, there is no speaker
Aye, there's the rub
I'm afraid, I'll just have to
Disappear over the PUB

WHEN WALKING DIED

They used to hang the washing out, the weather always fine
With pride for the whiteness displayed upon the line
Steps were polished and windows sparkled clean
Neighbours chatted freely, and told of where they'd been
Yet now the grass is never cut and graffiti is obscene
Life is now, so misconstrued
That if you cut your neighbours grass
You are liable to be sued
No dangers then, when walking in the city or the park
No talk of rape, or muggings in the dark
Now surrounded by road rage, locked inside your car
Do you wonder, if life has gone too far
Which day was it ?
The people cried
The day when walking died ?

CENTRE PARC BREAKS

Bruised, damaged, deaf from water flume
Yet no complaints
Sport's just great, as is the room
One small measure of regret
For as you get older, you simply forget
The energy of kids, offsets the "childish spell"
Are they ever quiet? Do they always yell !
Babies crying, toddlers tantrum
Teenagers sulk and romances blossom
From Leicester to Perth
Whilst adults exhausted, on their knees
Smile bravely
Praying for five minutes peace

CONE TODAY, GONE TOMORROW

Motorway traffic, all in a stew
Endless vehicles, in a queue
Onward ever onward, trying to press
Headaches forming, all from stress
Give an inch, steal a metre
Oh, for a helicopter, a single seater
Yet one point, never fails to amaze
As we peer through catalytic haze
What causes all these cars to stop?
What actually catches them on the hop?
For time will pass, and we will cheer
When cones and queue, just disappear

FORWARD

Birmingham Knockers on the Worlds door
Found every place, but never sure
Negative. "It can't be done!"
Yet do it, better than most
No wonder the motto "Forward"
For there is no way back
To minds and bodies founded on a thousand trades

Birmingham, a town of knockers
Self depreciation from each lip
On every shoulder a healthy chip
Each deal, always a bargain
"Oi've got a mate, who knows"

Pride and care, in Brum it shows
City of workers, City of wit
Each job a challenge, for senses to pit
Your accent so cringing
Your powers so great
Lucky the man, with a Brummy for a Mate

No job too large, nor too small
If there is money to earn
They're right on the ball
All colours, all creeds
So proud of their deeds
Long may you continue
To spread the good seeds
Of Brummagem ethics
Hard work, common sense and good deeds

THOUGHTS ON TELLY

The tellies on, such a trap
Watching, just a load of crap
Violence, drugs, watching worlds trouble
Peoples lives, reduced to rubble

Flies on children, eyes all glazed
Nothing sickens, never amazed
Inoculated, immune. As through the glass
Visions of Horror, quickly pass

Terrible things that we see
Whilst we take another cup of tea
TV responsibility - There is no care
I doubt, even if it came with smell, blood and muck
The average viewer gives a fuck

So we get what we deserve
No standards, no quality, no reserve
In the future, maybe someone will recall
That TV was civilisations downfall

THE VILLAGE PUB
do they exist?

The village centre, the very hub
Of gossip, scandal, what's on where
And Who is Who
Stories of old, rumours anew
The man to dig your garden
To fix, to paint, fence, or repair.
The know - how, the skills reported there
The talk, the smoke, the clinking glass
Subject matter - Everything - scientific and crass
Pundits on every subject, large or small
Football, politics, the latest joke
Shared amongst the village folk
Seated in the very nub
Of life which is a village PUB

BEHIND THE BAR

"What's yours?" One for the road, Bottoms up
"Welcome stranger, come and sup
Tell us your tale, your family and life
All revealed, happiness and strife."
Strange the names, Barmaid - Landlord
Yet very apt, for little is barred
As each soul is revealed under the influence
Confessions flow, freer than in Church
Behind the bar, you listen and only beer dispense
For today's shoulder, listens and forgets
Tomorrow's problems best

REDUNDANCY OR WERSE

The phone rang at eight
A little noise to change your life and fate
Please meet me at ten
Where with the stroke of a pen
You discover that life's getting late

Redundancy, the new name for the 'sack'
Fifteen years' service, then the stab in the back
The cheque you get looks good
Till you translate it to transport and food
We're not spendthrifts, but you look at the past
"My God, How long will this last?"

Strange feelings, you cannot describe
At first gladness: at least you are free
Then sickness grabs your inside
As suddenly all you can see
Is a future with no job for me

"You'll look back in 12 months and be glad"
Said the bastard, who gave you no warning
Let's hope he is right
Though things now may be tight
Maybe a new era is dawning.........

CREATION & AFTER

In the beginning, God created the Earth
And all the animals that walked upon it
Then Jesus created the hope of eternal life
And Homo sapiens have fought over it ever since
Then America invented McDonalds and Coca Cola
And mankind ate itself into obesity

COMING OUT OF WINTER

Spring is here again
Apples dusted with a fragile blossom
Defy the March winds
The late springs frosts
The birds and bees in frantic action bent
Encouraged by the flowers and scent
Put behind them, winters gloom
And cleaning starts in every room

Stars gaze upon a fragile man

Black, are the skies tonight
Pierced by jewelled stars, so bright
Diamonds could not shine
As God's beauty, define
The trivialities of man
Controlled within a living span
Who are we to know or care
When God's universe we share
Concerned only with our daily pleasure
Man's futility, its only measure

Thoughts on America

American inventions, there must be a few?
We must give them credit, where it is due
But selling them, I have to say
Is the absolute American forte

Bell and his telephone
A means by which your never alone
Denim, the cloth for pants
Cold, rough, no need for ants
Baseball caps, all one size
Back to front or over your eyes
No style, no class, no head protection
Just an advert for a convention
McDonalds, Mr Kentucky and his chicken and chips
Just more grease to put on our hips
Mr Ford and his Model T
Polluting fumes for all to see
Tobacco, heroin and now cocaine
As we continue, more profane
Thoughts spring to my mind
What other doubtful pleasures can we find
Cinema pleasures where once an Indian bit the dust
Yet now all we see is pornography and lust
TV programmes, from documentary to Frazier
Can we really find anything crazier
Than all the world paying a fee
To follow the exploits of Dallas and NYPD
Superman, Batman and other he men
Can they compete with the Presidents semen
So we examine the curdled cream
Of the so called American Dream
STOP. Come on, your being unfair
There must be something good that we can share
It's just too easy to snipe and jeer
At jeans, baseball hats and freezing beer
For most folks obviously don't find it a joke
They actually enjoy hamburgers and Coke
So my lonely path I must tread
With bowler, warm beer, good cheese and bread
Your finest achievements, I'll simply acknowledge
Not for you salt and porridge
And I'm certain that, very soon
You will find a reason for putting a man on the moon

LAS VEGAS

Blind, they sit
Driven by need
Lost is the cause
For greed is the seed
Vegas, bright lights, gamblers and porn
The dollar your harvest
The quarter your corn
City of wealth
City of sorrow
Such a strange place
But we'll be back tomorrow !!!!!!!

The Glasgow holiday train

Mother's time is always there
Loving, thoughtful, enough to share
Each child taking time and life
From women in their prime
Love given for ever
Love torn from the womb
Love that men can never know
Time given without reward
Giving life, ever forward
Time will tell and children go
Never looking back, it is so
Mother's love rejected, unnoticed
Until another seed is planted
The journey starts again

EXAMINATIONS

Two C's - Oh not two E's
What was the question?
Better to field the slings and arrows
Of outraged parents
Than to face the Board again

Did Shakespeare, the immortal Bard
Get the dreaded yellow card
Which sent him off, perchance to sleep
Or was it just for pinching sheep?
That left, that yawning, gaping void
That stretches forever in our youth

Without A's or B's, C, D or E's
How did we as parents survive
All those years, with hopes alive
Without those so important letters?
That are supposed to make us equal or betters
Can we survive? - their urgent plea
Without an A level and then a degree !!

Yet still, we live
Its all perspective
Who is happier ? Man or Mouse?
Life continues despite the grouse
And you will find along life's way
That a smile, a laugh and common sense
Will more than adequately recompense
For any degree or number of letters
It's love and laughter, that cast off fetters
Just look at life and do your best
Live for every moment, and never, rest
For you will find, in whatever genre
The other mans grass is always greener

BEST MANS STORY

Marriage is for when you find
A lover to share your life and mind
A friend who without a doubt
You cannot, possibly, live without
Someone who will love and care
Be upset, when you are not there
Someone who makes you laugh
Maybe serious, may be daft.
You don't care, there is no reason
When Cupids arrows are in season
So to you here on your Wedding Day
A little advice, to measure and weigh
"How can you measure Love? Pounds, feet or litres"
Love, cannot be checked, there are no meters
Like a car, sometimes fast, sometimes slow
But without some fuel, it sure won't go!
Don't worry, the fuel is cheap
Kisses. Morning, noon, and before you sleep
A kiss and a cuddle, I'm sure I can say
Will keep Love and Marriage, running for ever and a day

Christmas

Supermarket trollies, all overloaded
Alka Seltzer for tummies exploded
Coping with small children's petulance
With diaphragm strained and flatulence
Families gathered once a year
Exchanging the news and make good cheer
Cars overloaded with Christmas Presents
Good Old Santa to dispense
Ties & Nighties, dressing gown and socks
Computers toys, unreadable books
Xmas wrappings so lovingly tended
Soon in refuse sack and dustbin ended
Turkey with gravy, Turkey with stuffing
Turkey sandwich, Turkey creole
Turkey curry, Turkey with chips
All descending on those expanding hips
Do you suppose
There is no ending to that Parsons Nose?
Christmas games, when everyone cheats
Brand new socks, to clothe the feet
The morning after, which we all dread
Did we actually need that last Scotch before bed?
Glory to God, the excuse for a binge
Though Santas beard we occasionally singe
But never forget. This Festival of Fun
Was only made possible by the birth of a Son
Who taught us all, that love and giving
Is nearly as important as FORGIVING.

A FAIRY LIGHTS TALE

Most of the year, life's a bore
For fairy lights, stuck in a drawer
There they lie, gathering dust
Trying hard, not to get bust
Then Xmas arrives and all the family
Go to the Nursery for the tree
Where arguments soon range free
Over which one, has the perfect symmetry
Off to the attic, find the decorations
Getting things ready for the celebrations
Just one thought that we don't need
But the Devil must plant his seed
Some ones always bound to say
"I know they were working, when we put them away"
"Plug in the lights", the kids will urge
And fairy lights get an electric surge
"Ouch!, Ooh, Wow", our lights all glow
As weary elements go on show
Then they'll wink and they'll shine
Right up to Xmas Eve, all will be fine
But, when all is still and drinks in hands
Listening to carols played by Brass bands
Our lovely lights will just - GO OUT.
Dad will curse, Mom will fret
For it is, an odds on bet
That no matter how many spares you use
A spark of life will quite refuse
To appear, until all decorations are re-arranged
And every last bulb has been changed
So the Fairy Light Curse comes true
Every year - and - nothing new

Just a Fir-y Treet at Christmas time

A Fir cone fell on to the ground
And by a squirrel quickly found
Was buried with indecent haste
In a most secret, hidden place

Came the spring and in his ardour
The squirrel quite forgot his larder
Then with some warmth and a little rain
Our fur cone's, life cycle began again

Years passed by and quite plain to see
Our cone grew into a lovely tree
Whose branches tried, to rise so far
In a vain attempt to reach a star

Soon our tree was fully grown
Like a king upon a throne
Yet wishing with all his might
That he could reach the twinkling light

Then one day as he stood erect
A young man came and did select
The tree with a special sign
And from now on our story's fine

For with roots and all, our tree was taken
Nothing broken, nothing shaken
To stand most nobly, head in the air
In a place called Trafalgar Square

Now at Christmas, standing so tall
The tree, decorated, admired by all
With lights entwined, seen even from afar
This tree is now, its own Top Star
And just maybe in Fairyland
Our squirrel and his merry band
Swells with pride, and on the phone
Tells all his friends of this champion cone